MW01166545

But God, I'm So Humble Already

But God, I'm So Humble Already

Aletha Gruzensky Pineda

REVIEW AND HERALD® PUBLISHING ASSOCIATION
WASHINGTON, DC 20039-0555
HAGERSTOWN, MD 21740

The author assumes full responsibility for the accuracy of all facts and
quotations as cited in this book.

This book was
Edited by Raymond H. Woolsey
Designed by Bill Kirstein

Type set: Zapf Book Light

PRINTED IN U.S.A.

95 94 93 92 91 90   10 9 8 7 6 5 4 3 2 1

R & H Cataloging Service

Pineda, Aletha Louise (Gruzensky), 1952–
   But God, I'm so humble already.

   1. Humility. I. Title.
      301.11

ISBN 0-8280-0558-3

DEDICATION

To my father,
who in one two-minute conversation
changed my view of humility.

Acknowledgments

My husband, Bill, has been my encourager and critic. He was the one who decided we needed a computer and who suggested I cut down on other work in order to spend more time writing (and cooking more meals at home). Connie Nowlan and Sadie Engen read the manuscript and made suggestions. Dwight Nelson gave me a five-minute Greek lesson. To these I am grateful.

Most of the names of people in this book have been changed. Some details have been altered to protect individuals from recognition. However, the underlying points of the illustrations are true. Where real names are used, the individuals have given their permission in writing.

Contents

Preface

"Dad," I asked, "what has been your most humiliating experience? I'd like to write something about being humble."

He thought about that for a moment. "I think there's a big difference between being humiliated and being humble," he said. "A person can be humble without being humiliated."

I pondered that for a while. In fact, I pondered that for several years. He had not answered my query, but it was not important anymore. I began to question the concept of humility I had heard most often—that humility was synonymous with wormlike attitudes and feelings, that humility was passive, submissive, without thought, bland.

If God is love and wants the best for me while asking me to be humble, how, I asked, does humility relate to more positive aspects of life, such as value and love? How could humility help in developing the unique potential God gives each person?

This book is for anyone who, like me, has become discouraged with the idea that God teaches us humility by grinding us into the dirt. It is for anyone who wants to believe that anything God asks, any character trait He gives, makes us better and more fulfilled people.

HUMILITY AND SELF

Chapter 1

"But God, I'm So Humble Already . . ."

"Clothe yourselves with humility toward one another."
—1 Peter 5:5

"THIS course would really be useful overseas," Erik said, shoving a catalog across the library table.

I looked up, smiling. There was something about this guy. "Sounds interesting," I said, reading the lines he indicated. That's all it took for Erik to start talking about the developing country where he had worked before coming to study for an advanced degree. These discussions were becoming more frequent. I looked forward to them. Not only did I learn from him, but I enjoyed his attention. I sensed that he enjoyed our talks too.

As a child I had dreamed of being a missionary. Two years overseas had almost convinced me that Third World countries did not need "grass roots" missionaries anymore. But now Erik unfolded a part of the world with health, nutrition, and spiritual needs in villages that were accessible only by foot.

I was intrigued and excited. Maybe this friendship would be something more . . . well, maybe.

Then the blow fell. I remembered his words—kind but final. "You know, Aletha, I have felt like there is something developing between us. I intended nothing more than friendship. I enjoy your friendship, but I am not ready for a deeper relationship right now."

"That's OK," I said, but I felt the blood rush to my cheeks as I turned to go. I had let down my usual guard of shyness and had responded to his interest with enthusiasm. I felt like a puppy following the good smell of meat in a bag, only to have the bag whisked away to the freezer.

I could find no logical reason to help ease the pain. Both of us were working on advanced degrees. He was nearly finished. He had even casually brought up the subject of marriage in a general sense as we talked.

Often I had heard Christians say that God sends trials to develop humility. One Christian preacher had told of a time when he had asked God to keep him humble. God had answered his prayers the very next day, he said, by allowing people to question his abilities and threaten his job.

As a Christian, I wanted to be humble. However, now humiliation seemed to wash over me like crashing, breaking waves pulling me out with the undertow.

"But God," I prayed, "I'm so humble already."

Then I stopped short. Only proud people prayed like that. Or did they? Was this really humility?

Was humility a head hung low, suffering embarrassment or wrongs? Did it mean taking any kind of abuse? Or was it something different?

As I thought of God's love, it didn't make sense for Him to use humiliation to teach humility. To me, humiliation seemed more a product of sin, the result of faulty communication, the aftermath of poor choices or choices that had to be made without all the facts. Humiliation threatened my inner existence and even my belief in God.

Months passed before I realized that humility would enable me to deal with humiliation. A humble attitude would help me to live in a less-than-perfect world full of less-than-perfect choices, decisions, and people.

With my guilt over not being humble enough now gone, I could allow humility to help me in several ways:

1. Humility widened my perceptions. I saw that humiliating experiences come to all—proud and humble alike. Knowing that almost everyone is rejected at some time in life took some of the sting out of my experience. How could I expect my life to go perfectly when no one else's did?

2. Humility helped me save the good from my friendship with Erik. God had planned that friendship for a reason. Humility helped me accept God's reason in place of my preconceived ideas.

I had learned. I had been challenged. That growth did not disappear because my hopes for the future would not work out. I did not have to set up blocks against everything the friendship offered.

3. Humility helped me give someone else the gift of freedom. Having accepted God's reason for the friendship, I also accepted God's plans for Erik's life. I did not know what was best for him or me, but love meant wanting that best for both of us. I could allow him to choose.

Humiliation hadn't made me humble. It had, however, given me an opportunity to use humility.

Humility opened the way to change my thoughts and expectations. I discovered that, rather than being a heavy burden destined to make us forever unhappy on this earth, humility was a friend.

Chapter 2

Toothpaste on My Razor

*"Humble me, humble me, O Lord.
Humble me so I can do Your will."*
—*Spiritual*

MIKE'S morning had gone poorly. One of the chemical reactions in the lab where he worked had boiled over, forcing him to start anew. While cleaning up the mess in the chemistry hood, he dropped a beaker, which shattered on the floor. He found the broom, but someone had borrowed the dustpan and not returned it to its place. He finally used a piece of cardboard.

Retreating to the office we shared for a much-earned break, Mike remembered that he had forgotten his lunch. He laughingly sighed, "I knew it was going to be a bad day when I put toothpaste on my razor this morning."

He paused until my laughter subsided. "I'm not going to let it get me down, though," he added.

I looked at Mike with new admiration. He could laugh at things that would frustrate me. Was this part of humility? I wondered.

With humility, everyday situations that do not go exactly right no longer signal the despair that comes from wounded pride or embarrassment. Instead, humility helps trigger laughter at the most humiliating circumstances.

I remembered one of my most humiliating times. I had just arrived in Australia and was surprised that the English language is spoken in so many different ways. I struggled to learn new names for many common things.

I thought I was doing quite well. Then Doris invited me for tea. Not being well acquainted with her group of friends, I politely listened to their chatter, which centered mostly on past activities unique to their group.

Right in the middle of eating all the good food, one of life's basic biological urges struck. I squirmed uncomfortably until Doris went into the kitchen to put the finishing touches on her chocolate mousse. I followed her to the kitchen.

In a hushed voice I asked, "Where is your restroom?"

"Restroom?" she practically yelled in her high-pitched voice. "We rest in bed."

"Yeah, well, the bathroom." I blushed a little.

"You want to take a bath?"

My face turned redder by the second.

She raised her voice another 10 decibels. "We call it the toilet!"

I heard the whole group in the next room explode with laughter as she pointed me to the proper room. And though a salty liquid in my eyes blurred my vision a little, I smiled and tried to laugh.

I would have liked to stay in "the toilet" for the rest of the evening. Instead, I waited until my tear ducts had absorbed the excess moisture. Then I slipped back to my place to listen quietly to chatter about their friends. I had made my one contribution to the evening.

I could not sincerely laugh at this experience right away. Being a stranger added to my sensitivity. I was so embarrassed that I had little desire to be around anyone in the group again.

Fortunately, one person, Colin, helped me over the hurdle to humor. By taking an interest and including me in the conversation, he helped me to feel comfortable.

A few days later I met Colin again. When he steered the conversation to the subject of words and their different meanings—including toilet versus bathroom—in different cultures, I knew he understood. Feeling accepted, I could laugh.

Colin's acceptance helped me take the long view. Everyone has a most embarrassing moment. Thinking about how that embarrassing incident might look 10 years later and how it might look to other people helped me laugh.

Laughter, in turn, helped me to accept myself even more. When the experience became funny, it no longer threatened to hurt me permanently.

A friend said that getting people to laugh at you can really be a service to others. The laughter can make people feel more comfortable and lighten a stiff conversation.

"I just need to brown this apple crisp a little," I said to my husband, Bill. "I promised to bring it for lunch tomorrow. I guess there's going to be quite a crowd."

"Why don't we sing a little while it's baking," Bill suggested. "I'll get out our guitars."

"Humble me, humble me, O Lord. Humble me so I can . . . ' "

"What's that I smell?"

I jumped up. "Oh, no. The crisp." I ran to the oven, where smoke rose from the top of the closed door. Pulling the door open, I jerked the crisp out.

"It's ruined," I said, looking at the blackened topping and thinking of the time involved in making another apple crisp.

"It can't be ruined," Bill said as he struggled to see through billows of smoke and hurried to open the door.

Painstakingly I scraped off the burned topping. Later, with a new topping, the crisp again looked presentable.

"There," I said. "I don't think anyone will know what has happened."

"Would you mind if I told about this tomorrow at lunch?" Bill asked. "I mean, if the situation is right."

"Please don't."

"But it's so funny, and everyone will get a kick out of it. 'Humble me, humble . . . What's that I smell?' Suddenly I see you enveloped in clouds of smoke." We both broke out laughing.

"OK, you can tell it, but please wait until people have eaten at least half of it. I don't want anyone to have smoky preconceived ideas of its flavor."

Conversation at dinner the next day lagged just slightly. Two doctors sat at one end of the table discussing medicine. Others politely asked and answered questions.

"This looks good," the hostess remarked, serving up the dessert.

Inwardly I breathed a sigh of relief.

"Can I tell them about the crisp now?" Bill asked.

"Not yet," I replied.

"She doesn't want us to know that all she uses are wormy apples," a guest said.

"No, it's not that bad," I said. "Go ahead and tell them, Bill."

I felt a little blood rush to my cheeks as Bill repeated the story, but I laughed with everyone else. I relaxed even more when I noticed that no one had stopped eating the apple crisp.

And Bill pointed out afterward, "Did you notice how people started talking after I told that story? The discussion got lively. They just needed something like that to relax and start talking."

Humility had helped me let others see my mistake in a humorous way. The humor helped them feel more comfortable.

Chapter 3

Worm or Butterfly?

"Each one should test his own actions. Then he can take pride in himself."—Galatians 6:4

YOU'RE just a little mouse."

I looked at my friend astride her bike. Not knowing what else to say, as usual, I said, "Well, I had a good ride. See you."

I rode up my driveway and went inside to look in the mirror. Did she mean my looks, my quietness, or my lack of aggressiveness when it came to doing the things she told me she'd done? Maybe I was more like a worm—a slithery little entity that got little attention and was even stepped on occasionally. Objectively, I did not need to worry. Some people who knew me thought I had a lot going for me. It was not the way I felt, though.

Mouse. Worm. Neither sounded good. In fact, they both felt the same—bad. Nevertheless, I had high expectations for college. I had not dated much in high school, and someone told me, "Don't worry. Just wait until you get to college. The guys will be tired of the girls who are popular now. You'll have a lot of dates in college."

My first weekend at college, I excitedly wondered who would ask me out. No one? Oh, well. Maybe the second weekend. No? What was wrong?

Guys just were not jangling my phone the way I'd hoped. As dateless weekend followed dateless weekend, my spirits and hopes dropped lower and lower.

One of my friends from high school had given me some advice. "Read this book," she said. "It really tells you how to relate to men."

I had looked at her bright eyes and blonde curls. I had seen guys enthralled with her attention, oblivious to their surroundings. She had dates. I could not deny the evidence.

The book said that men had big egos, which successful women were supposed to feed. Maybe guys would like me better if I never did anything really well. Then they would feel superior.

Now at college, I determined to try even harder to follow the book's advice. I actively hid any good thing about myself that I thought might threaten a sensitive male ego. My grades dropped. I shied away from conversations about anything I enjoyed doing if I was afraid that a guy did not know much about that subject.

The results? Still no dates. I felt consistently uptight and depressed. This was not fun at all. If I had owned the book, I would have burned it.

School wasn't what I'd expected either. Teachers did not seem to know I was there. Other students made bright, intelligent comments in class. I wondered what I was doing there. Finally I swallowed a little of the pride that told me only insecure wimps told others their problems. I made an appointment to talk with one of my professors.

My stomach tightened into a hard knot as I walked toward his office. By the time I walked into the building, I had to dash to the bathroom to try to control the dinner threatening to take a detour.

Finally I sat in Ron's office (he insisted we call him by his first name). "I feel like a number here," I said. "I go here, go there. Do what I'm supposed to do. No one seems to care."

"Tell me a little about yourself."

"Well, there's not much to tell, really. I've always been quite shy, never really popular or anything. I don't really seem to find life that meaningful. One of my friends recently attempted suicide. Sometimes I wonder what keeps me from doing the same." I paused, thinking.

I omitted the fact that I had been my high school valedictorian, a member of both band and choir, National Honor Society treasurer, and had worked to pay off a sizable amount of my school bill. The way I was feeling, all these achievements did not seem to matter anymore.

Moments passed. The silence was not exactly uncomfortable, just silent.

Then Ron spoke. "You know . . . tell me if I'm right . . . I don't think you like yourself very well. Many people don't. They try to hide everything about themselves, hoping that people will like them better."

"Hmmm," I said. "You may be right."

"In reality, the more people know about you, the better they will like you. You are a unique person. God made you unique. That uniqueness makes you valuable."

"Sometimes it feels more like 'weird' than 'valuable,' " I said quietly. But I thought, *Why hasn't anyone ever told me that uniqueness means value? I wonder if I really am valuable?*

"You can accept yourself. We all have strengths and weaknesses—every single person. You can even accept mistakes you might make. They are what make you human."

I looked at him, speechless. How did he know that I always tried to do my best, and took it hard when I did not match up to my standards of perfection or what I thought others expected from me?

"It's like when you go skiing. Sometimes you fall down. You don't lie there moaning about the fact that you fell down. You get up and ski on down the hill. Next time you'll do something different when you come to that spot on the slope."

"That makes sense," I said, smiling as a relaxed feeling suddenly swept over me. I would have to think about these things.

"You have a neat smile," he said as he opened the door for me to leave.

If he thought I had a neat smile, maybe I should smile more. Life started to get better as I gradually allowed myself to be who I was, doing the things I enjoyed and did well.

When I could appreciate myself, I found I could appreciate others. I could converse with genuine concern about things important to them because I cared and was interested. I could talk to guys just for the fun of talking. And eventually dates came too.

My thinking about Christianity started changing also. I began to see God as a loving being who really cared about me, rather than a dictator demanding perfection. Instead of standing ready to zap me with humiliation whenever I became proud, God waited, ready to help me when I came to Him with my needs.

Like me, many people have a hard time liking or accepting themselves. Society demands perfection. Parents, employers, and spouses add expectations. Even the church has high standards to be upheld.

My inability to match up to my own or others' expectations resulted in a damaged self-esteem. Even if I could match up, as I had done in previous years, I could not feel good about it, because that would have been pride. No one had told me that self-esteem and pride are not the same. According to S. J. Sundeen and associates, most people try to increase self-esteem in one of two ways, illustrated by the following model. [1]

This model, according to Sundeen, will allow for two ways to increase self-esteem: take away from either the real self or ideal self.

Self-esteem goes up if one lowers expectations for the ideal self. The ideals are not as high and one has more success in living up to them. The success increases self-esteem.

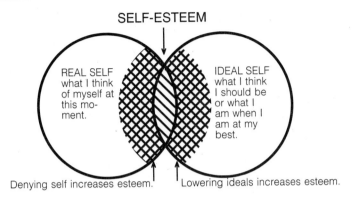

SELF-ESTEEM

REAL SELF
what I think
of myself at
this mo-
ment.

IDEAL SELF
what I think
I should be
or what I
am when I
am at my
best.

Denying self increases esteem. | Lowering ideals increases esteem.

A person can also increase esteem by covering up or hiding the real self through the powerful psychological defense mechanism of denial. A person using denial usually does not know it. Only others can see the vast difference between the real self and the way the individual thinks of himself.

A classic example of a person using denial is an alcoholic who cannot see the problems his habit causes himself or others. The denial allows him to keep some self-esteem or raise his self-esteem above what it would be if he viewed himself as an alcoholic. Humility, when seen correctly, actually offers a third way of increasing self-esteem. Instead of either denying the real self or lowering ideals, humility allows an honest look at the real self.

At first, that honest look would seem to lower self-esteem, since the real self may be very different from the ideal self. But humility includes acceptance of that real self. Only in seeing the real self can one even begin to change in the direction of the ideal self.

That change, with the help of God, increases self-esteem. Interacting with others, increasing knowledge, and discovering new ideas all open up areas for growth. Growing toward goals increases self-esteem.

Humility allows me to recognize the difference between the real self and the ideal self. I do not need to put a lower value on myself just because the real self and ideal self do

SELF ESTEEM

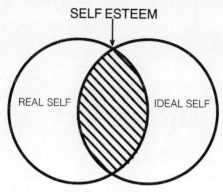

REAL SELF   IDEAL SELF

not match. Instead, humility helps me to accept the person that I am at the moment.

Finally, I know I am valuable because God loves and values me. God, in Jesus Christ, died to bridge that gap between real self and ideal self. In fact, Christ closed the gap. In a relationship with me, He actually sees the potential He created in me. He sees the finished product before it is finished.

Self-concept grows most when nourished by a deepening knowledge of God's love. A biography of Christ contains these words:

"The Lord is disappointed when His people place a low estimate upon themselves. He desires His chosen heritage to value themselves according to the price He has placed upon them. God wanted them, else He would not have sent His Son on such an expensive errand to redeem them." [2] Value for self comes not because of self greatness, but because of what Christ has done. Esteeming self shows appreciation for the gift of a redeemed life.

Does this value of self negate humility? No. I know my value comes from an undeserved gift: re-creating my life in the image of God. In God's hands, worms become butterflies.

---

[1] From S. J. Sundeen et al., *Nurse-Client Interaction: Implementing the Nursing Process,* 2nd. ed. (St. Louis: The C. V. Mosby Co., 1981), p. 247.

[2] Ellen G. White, *The Desire of Ages* (Mountain View, Calif.: Pacific Press Publishing Assn., 1940), p. 668.

Chapter 4

Dreaming Big

"Humble yourselves before the Lord, and He will lift you up."—James 4:10

I HAD tuned in to the droning radio preacher to keep me awake through the endless stretch of Nebraska highway. At 2:00 in the morning, he was just barely doing the job.

"You've got to have a dream bigger than you are."

The thought jolted me awake. Was he talking to me? I recalled the events of the past few months. Small events, and yet I had wondered about them.

I had not known much about Papua New Guinea. It sounded as though it might be somewhere in Africa or, well . . . where?

Suddenly, though, everywhere I went I seemed to be confronted by the needs of this large island north of Australia. One day as I walked through the library, a book caught my eye. Taking it off the shelf, I discovered it was about Papua New Guinea. This happened twice.

I went to a lecture, only to hear Papua New Guinea mentioned. A friend started talking to me about Papua New Guinea and its culture—even though he had never been there. Papua New Guinea seemed to be mentioned everywhere.

As the white dashes on the pavement of Interstate 80 flashed by, I began to wonder. Was God trying to tell me something? Was this my dream—a dream bigger than I am? Could I do anything at all to help improve the health of the people in Papua New Guinea? Until now the idea had seemed so preposterous that I had not dared to think about it. But with nothing to do except make sure the car kept going toward Colorado, I had time to think about both the possibilities and the problems.

Parts of this large island had had contact with the Western world for only 30 years. The tribes, living in a mostly mountainous area roughly the size of Colorado, spoke more than 700 different languages. Simply communicating might be hard.

The life span of an average man at that time was about 48 years. Malnutrition robbed children of vitality. Alcohol stole lives and wrecked cars. A new car lasted, on the average, only about 18 months.

The seeds of the dream continued to grow. A year later I went to Papua New Guinea. If solutions to problems are to be permanent, the people must solve their own problems. I wanted to be a catalyst to help the people of that country solve their problems—a resource and support person with information and a means of communicating that information.

I encountered problems from the moment I arrived. God solved some of those problems. Some were never solved. When my time there ended, the dream still loomed bigger than I. Someone else would have to carry on.

Is dreaming big a part of humility? The actual act of going to Papua New Guinea did not seem to be particularly humble. I went rather excited about the possibilities.

Following through on dreams, though, and making reality out of thoughts involves some risk. Humility frees me to take that risk. I can accept my humanity and limitations.

Humility means that even achieving less than total success will not halt my efforts. I am free to dream big. I am free to keep on trying to make reality of the dreams.

Dr. Richard Douce, a Christian physician, once stated, "As I meditate on Scripture, it seems to me that God is much more interested in faithfulness than productivity. You hear of missionaries who labor for years without one person coming to Christ. God can change that in an instant—when the time is right. The important thing is that they were faithful in doing their job."

I left Papua New Guinea feeling that I had not finished my task. Later I realized that if He wanted to, God could take the little that I had done and multiply it as He had done for the boy who brought Jesus five loaves and two fishes (Matthew 14:17). Or God could choose to do nothing. And that's humbling.

Humility is a natural consequence of accepting responsibility for a task just a little beyond our reach. Humility is not the primary goal. Yet humility comes in attempts to make a positive impact on the world.

Being willing to take risks puts a whole new light on James's advice to "humble yourselves before the Lord, and he will lift you up" (James 4:10).

If when reading this passage I think in terms of behavior, I go to God with a list of all my humble actions and ask that He fulfill His part of the bargain. I am in control. I have done my duty, and now it is time for the reward. But I wait forever.

In contrast, if when reading "humble" in James I think in terms of attitude, then I come to God with an emptiness to be filled. I present to Him my lack of knowledge in a certain area, or the need for more ability to accomplish some task.

Then God hears and answers. He increases talents or knowledge. He gives wisdom and insight to deal with people. In fact, He will give whatever I need to do good. By filling the need, God has lifted me up to greater ability.

Leland Kaiser, a professor at the University of Colorado Graduate School of Business, said something about humility when he told an audience how to increase their talents.

"Do you want to know how to get a new talent?" He paused as anticipation grew. "Take on a task that you can't do. Take on a task that's bigger than you are."

"Do you know what happens then?" He paused again. "God looks down and sees a human being slugging it out for all he's worth, trying to accomplish something good. And God says, 'There's My person having a pretty rough time. I think I'll help out.'

"And plunk. God drops down a new talent."

When I was in Papua New Guinea and needed some illustrations for a pamphlet on alcohol, I remembered what Kaiser had said. I knew I'd never be able to take the right photos.

Someone had told me that the Papua New Guineans related well to cartoons. That's what I needed, I decided. But where could I find the right ones? Who could do it? I was not a cartoonist.

"God," I prayed, "I've heard Leland Kaiser say that You are willing to drop down new talents when we need them to accomplish some good. I need some cartoon figures right now. I've never drawn a cartoon before. Please help me."

I got out some local newspapers and studied the cartoons. The people had to look like Papua New Guineans, not like Europeans. Spreading out a sheet of paper, I began to draw.

My supervisor saw the pamphlet the next day. His eyes opened in surprise when he saw the cartoons. "Those are pretty good," he said.

"Thank You, God," I said in my heart.

While the cartoons may not have been perfect, God had given something more than I'd had before. In going to God with my needs, humility had become a tool to success.

HUMILITY AND OTHERS

▼

Chapter 5

Practicing Humility— Enjoyable?

"Clothe yourselves with compassion, kindness, humility, gentleness and patience."—Colossians 3:12

TODAY we are going to learn how to fall," Pat announced, fingering her whistle, her sign of authority as a physical education teacher. She pointed to the tumbling mats.

Falling didn't sound like the fun-and-games physical education class I had expected when I signed up. But I lined up with the other students.

"Someday, like it or not, you are going to fall," Pat continued. "Most people fall straight out, catching themselves with their hands and possibly breaking a wrist. That's wrong. Fall on your side—like this."

She made it look simple.

"Now, fall."

We did.

"Again."

Amazingly, this wasn't too bad. In fact, it was almost fun. I had never fallen before without getting hurt.

Pat blew her whistle. "Landing on your head when you fall could leave you paralyzed. If you feel one of those falls coming, twist around and roll off your shoulder." She demonstrated.

As we practiced I found myself bouncing up from falls as though nothing had happened. I felt my confidence increasing as my fear of falling disintegrated.

Practicing humility, too, could increase confidence. An attitude learned when things are going well, under relatively safe conditions, could serve as a safety net to prevent serious injury in times of trial, humiliation, or embarrassment.

Here's the problem, though. Many people think that practicing humility means becoming submissive, passive, a nonachiever. These people think that to be humble, they have to wear old clothes, walk with a slump, or be employed in a job that will not pay enough to cover even the barest living expenses.

But that's not true. These actions may even signal false humility—behaviors worn on the outside like an old coat, mere behaviors related to no one but self.

True humility broadens horizons, opens the mind to new thoughts, and helps people creatively reach the potential God intended. True humility also helps in dealing with the falls and pain of a sinful world when they do come.

True humility permeates all attitudes toward others. Humility is a way of relating to people, considering them on every level. Humility must develop in the context of other people.

C. H. Spurgeon said, "I believe every Christian . . . has a choice between being humble and being humbled. . . . If you do not choose to be humble you will have to be humbled, and that is not at all a desirable thing." *

We can learn humility the way many children learn to fall in the rough-and-tumble games of childhood. However, God may have to teach us by "blowing His whistle" and telling us to practice. What Spurgeon forgot to add is that, in His love, God provides tumbling mats and will even tell us how to fall if we will listen.

God can teach us even when we are in the middle of a trial, unlike the physical education teacher, who would not be able to teach correct falling patterns while the fall is in progress.

However, His very character of love says that He would rather teach humility before any trials come. He would rather use more positive circumstances and ways that will benefit, even during the learning. Practicing humility under His safe conditions might even be somewhat enjoyable.

---

* C. H. Spurgeon, *Twelve Sermons on Humility* (London: Passmore & Alabaster), p. 533.

Chapter 6

Can I Help the Way I Feel?

"See to it . . . that no bitter root grows up to cause trouble."
—Hebrews 12:15

W E'VE hired Laurie part-time at work."
Beth felt her stomach tighten. That was the job she had applied for several months ago. She had been told that she would be the next person hired if they needed anyone.

"Why her?" Beth asked. She grabbed her coat. "I'm going for a walk."

She strode briskly down the road. "She moves to town, marries Bob, a doctor, and instantly has popularity—and now a job."

She thought about how people swarmed around to welcome Laurie. Beth would have welcomed her too if given a chance. But even though she and Bob had been friends before, he had introduced Laurie to everyone but Beth.

She had watched Laurie in her furry coat discussing color analysis, and wondered if they had anything in common anyway. No use in even introducing herself. What would they talk about? Now Laurie had "her" job. It wasn't fair. Every encounter with Laurie, even though indirect, seemed to scream at Beth, "You're no good."

"Does marrying a doctor make her any better than the rest of us?" Beth fumed as she walked. "Does that give her special privileges? Apparently it does. Doesn't getting this job prove it?"

As the walk worked off her surge of adrenalin, she started thinking more rationally. She knew Laurie did not intend to put her down or take "her" job. How could she if she did not even know Beth existed? Laurie could not be blamed for the way Beth felt. Beth stopped and looked at the sky. "God, I can't help the way I feel right now. I'm willing for You to change my feelings. I know You can do it. In fact, You are going to have to do it, because I can't."

She kicked a stone and watched as it tore through the weeds by the side of the road. "But I don't want to be bitter or hold a grudge. Please help me. Show me what to do."

As she walked toward home, Beth felt impressed that to change her feelings she needed to do something positive for Laurie. *A rose.* The thought leaped into her mind.

That's ridiculous, her logical side countered. *Why should I give her a rose?* But the thought persisted.

Rose in hand, Beth sat in her car for several minutes, alternating between glancing at Laurie's door and staring at the steering wheel. What should she say? "Here is a rose. 'Bye."

Or should she say something like "I'm having a hard time liking you—even though I don't know you, you robber. But here is this rose because I want to feel good, positive feelings toward you"? No. Too honest.

Slowly she got out of the car. Her knees felt weak. Her hands shook a little. But she forced herself to walk across the street and up the drive. This was agony. She slowly pushed the doorbell.

Laurie answered, wearing blue jeans, which at that moment was decidedly in her favor.

"I brought you something," Beth said holding out the flower.

"How lovely," Laurie said. "What's the occasion?"

Beth breathed a sigh of relief when Laurie invited her in without waiting for an answer. Sitting in the living room, she listened as Laurie talked about past jobs and her hometown. Beth discovered they both liked small towns and both were interested in helping people.

With new perceptions, Beth had a new set of feelings, based on an appreciation of Laurie for who she was. Beth had grown beyond her loss of the job and feelings of insignificance.

Humility helped Beth handle an emotionally charged situation when she recognized that feelings can change. Feelings do not necessarily define a situation, nor are they set in concrete.

Feelings often come spontaneously. Adrenalin surges. Hormones flow. Past experiences add color. Lack of sleep or a bad meal influences feelings. Even an inherited brain structure can dictate perceptions.

People often say, "I can't help the way I feel." That is true, but we can choose whether to keep the feelings. Humility gives the option of changing those feelings with God's help.

Chapter 7

Forgive? What For?

"Be kind and compassionate . . . forgiving each other just as in Christ God forgave you."—*Ephesians 4:32*

JON stood in shock as he watched Lisa, the girl he had been dating, pull away from the curb in a car with Doug. He felt a numbness start in his head and move downward. His knees felt like Jello, his feet like lead.

Were the rumors true after all? He had heard that Lisa and Doug were living together. Jon had decided that his informer seemed bitter about past experiences with Lisa. The rumors sounded like an attempt to get even.

Jon decided that trust must be part of any relationship. He would be cautious, but his values dictated that he trust Lisa. He could not pronounce her guilty without evidence. Now watching Lisa and Doug drive away, he wondered if his trust had been in vain.

He had to talk with Lisa. He had to find out for sure. At home he hesitated before punching the numbers on the phone with his index finger. He took two deep breaths, listening for the ring. At her "Hello" he tried to clear the tightness out of his throat as he spoke.

"Could we get together sometime soon? There's something we need to talk about."

"Well, how about during lunch hour tomorrow?" Lisa replied. The next day at lunch Jon asked her how her day was going. They talked about the weather.

Finally Lisa said, "What's on your mind?"

"I don't really know how to talk about this," Jon said.

"How about the straight approach?" Lisa suggested.

"Well, OK. Umm . . . Is it true that you and Doug are living together? I mean, I've heard that you are, and I saw you driving away together last night."

There was silence for a moment. Finally Lisa spoke.

"Yes, he is living at my place. But no, we aren't exactly living together. He house sat for me when I was gone and just hasn't moved out yet. He'll be getting his own apartment next week."

"But you did date him at one time?"

"Yes, but that was before you. He has another girlfriend now. In fact, they'll probably get married."

Knowing the truth helped only slightly. Somehow it didn't seem quite right—quite fair to him—quite something. He still didn't really understand the rationale behind having a former boyfriend living at her house while she dated someone else.

As he drove home the numbness settled somewhere in Jon's stomach. Questions and emotions pitched back and forth in his mind. Why had he trusted? Why hadn't he checked out the rumors sooner? What should he do now?

He slammed on the brakes and stopped inches from the back bumper of another car. Stunned, Jon realized he had been too busy thinking. He couldn't keep this up. "I need a solution, God," he said aloud, while looking at the traffic light.

Jon remembered an incident in the life of Corrie ten Boom. When one of Corrie's tormentors from a German concentration camp had asked her for forgiveness, she had felt utterly incapable of forgiving. But she told God that she would go through the actions if He would supply the feeling.

As Corrie reached out to shake the man's hand, a warm tingling started in her arm, and feelings of love welled up inside her. God had given her the forgiveness she needed to give.

"God," Jon prayed, "I know I have the right to be angry, if for no other reason than because Lisa hid crucial information from me. Some people in this situation would never speak to her again."

Jon paused, thinking. "But I've discovered, and You already know, that bitterness is my worst enemy. Can You give me the kind of forgiveness You gave Corrie ten Boom?"

Jon turned into his driveway and went inside. He pulled out a piece of paper and began to write. He paused as he concluded the letter and reread the last paragraph.

"Lisa, I won't deny that I am hurt. But I don't want that hurt to turn into bitterness. If you want forgiveness, I will forgive. I sensed as we talked that this whole business hasn't been easy for you, either. If you need a friend, you still have one in me."

When he saw her again, Lisa's face looked more relaxed as she took him aside. "Thank you so much for that letter," she said. "It was just what I needed. I thought for sure I would lose you as a friend by telling the truth."

Jon felt the numbness in his stomach melt away as she spoke. Would they keep on dating? He wasn't sure about that. But whatever happened with this relationship, he would keep positive emotions in his life, fighting against the bitterness that could destroy him.

Jon wanted to live out in his life the verse in Hebrews that says, "See to it that no one misses the grace of God and that no bitter root grows up to cause trouble and defile many" (Hebrews 12:15).

Lisa's response to Jon was something extra. His primary motive in writing the letter was to help change his own feelings—the only feelings he could directly control. His emotions were his responsibility.

Many people find forgiveness easier once the guilty person has groveled before them. They will extend a few words of forgiveness only when they think the guilty persons have punished themselves enough. They will make sure, though, that the guilty persons will never forget how indebted they are to the ones they hurt.

Real forgiveness, however, equalizes people. True forgiveness lets the guilty rise to the level of the one wronged. And not only when asked. Rather, true forgiveness changes feelings about the little things no one stops to mention.

Humility opens the way for that change, allowing God to transform emotions. In dealing with feelings in this way, pain heals, and relationships with other people strengthen.

Chapter 8

The Way I Perceive It . . .

"As we perceive, we feel."—Author unknown

I AWOKE from the dream clammy and sweating. The scene had been vivid—almost as if it had really happened. I had been a college community student again. I had hoped my boyfriend, who lived in the college dormitory, would invite me to a special Sunday morning breakfast to be held between 4:30 and 7:30 a.m.

But he did not even mention the breakfast. Since we had a good relationship, I thought about how pleased he would be if I just showed up to eat with him.

But then the doubts came. Had he not mentioned the breakfast because he thought I wouldn't be interested? Or had he not invited me because he didn't want me there?

The stage set now, I had to find out. At 7:20 a.m. I braved the cafeteria line to load my tray with blueberry-topped waffles, whipped cream, a bowl of applesauce, and a glass of orange juice.

Surveying the crowded dining room, I finally spotted my boyfriend eating with his roommate's girlfriend. Joyful anticipation mixed with anxiety twisted my stomach into knots as I walked toward them. I knew he was not interested in the other girl, but would he welcome me?

I set my tray on the table. He looked up sleepily. With a sneer on her face the girl said, "What are you doing here? You're late anyway." He said nothing.

Blink. Flash. Thud. My mixed feelings screamed "Rejection!" With a swoop of my arm I swung my tray. Dishes clattered all over the table, and blueberry goop covered them both. Carrying my empty tray, I dashed from the cafeteria, sobbing.

Not only had I been rejected, but I had also made a fool of myself, probably blowing our relationship for good. Nothing could calm my despair. I decided I could at least apologize and offer to talk things over.

Amazingly, my dream man said he'd come right over. And equally amazing, he was more calm, patient, and unperturbed than I would expect anyone to be after a dousing with blueberries. He listened while I explained the anxiety I had at coming at all, and how his silence and her apparent sarcasm spelled rejection to me.

"So you weren't really angry at me?" he said.

"Well, a little at the moment. I just couldn't handle being rejected."

"The breakfast was nothing special to me. I just needed to eat when the cafeteria was open. I figured you would probably rather sleep a little longer."

Relationship restored. I awoke to the sound of the alarm and a hug from the real man who in real life would neither give me cause for anxiety nor take blueberry splatterings with quite as much objectivity or patience.

Usually life is not this dramatic—or as easily fixed. In fact, I did not even know I was capable of throwing food at someone—even in my dreams. Usually I try to control my impulses, thinking only about what I would like to do to "that jerk."

What causes these misunderstandings? Before I act or feel, I perceive. I form images in my mind, based on the facts my senses relay to my brain. I make judgments about those facts.

Even before I imagine and judge, I expect some things to be a certain way, based on culture, upbringing, and past experiences. When perceptions of reality clash with expectations of what should be, I have problems. My perceptions of the facts dictate my feelings.

An elderly lady with a cane and thick-lensed glasses starts cautiously across the street. Suddenly a teenage boy dashes into the street, grabs her under the arms, and drags her toward the sidewalk, where another teenager waits.

What kind of feelings does this scene produce? Indignation? Outrage? Perhaps fear of teenage boys? We are probably glad when the lady grips her cane in surprise and attempts to hit the boy's shins.

Her heels bump along the blacktop and hit the curb with a thud; he finally manages to drag her up onto the sidewalk. At that moment a car swerves close, scraping against the curb and turning sharply down the wrong side of the road. The driver shouts an obscenity as he throws a bottle out the window.

Do your feelings change with added information? Now we may feel pride in such a quick-thinking teenager, or anger at the driver. The woman's anger and fear disappear immediately as she thanks the boy who has saved her life.

As perceptions change, feelings also change. Humility can help in taking active charge of perceptions. When humble, I realize that I do not know everything. Humility opens other ways of seeing things and gives a willingness to look through someone else's eyes.

New understanding helps solve problems and clear up misunderstandings. I can get all the facts. I can choose not to pass judgment based only on my past experiences. I can ask for information about motives or intentions.

I'm embarrassed as I remember the time my husband and I almost had a fight over wrinkled clothes. He had taken the laundry to wash and dry. I had come to pick it up.

Bill met me as I drove up. "The laundry is all folded and ready to go," he said hurriedly. "I'll bring it out. I've got to get to class."

"Wonderful," I said, looking at the folded towel on top. That was one less thing I would have to do immediately. Several hours later I finally had time to put away the clothes. I lifted off three folded towels and discovered a mountain of wrinkles below. Wrinkled baby dresses. Wrinkled sheets. Wrinkled towels.

"He lied to me," I fumed. "He just wanted to get out of doing the work. He wants to keep me chained to this house smoothing out wrinkles that shouldn't even be there in the first place."

Needless to say, with this view of the situation, I was furious—more furious than I care to really admit. We had guests coming that night, and since I did not want to stew about it all afternoon, I went to find Bill.

By the time I found him, I had cooled down enough to think that maybe we'd had a misunderstanding.

"Bill," I said, "did you intend to tell me all the clothes were folded?"

"What? Why?" he asked.

"They are all wrinkled. Everything. I thought they were folded, so I didn't rush to put them away."

"You came all the way over here to ask me about the clothes?"

"Well, yes. I'm angry, and I don't want to fume all afternoon. It just gets worse."

"In my rush to get to class and with my mind on a test, I guess I said the wrong thing. I meant to say that the clothes that needed to be hung were hung up," Bill said. "I'm glad you're here, though. I'd like your advice about something."

The anger suddenly melted away as I relaxed. My perception of his motives made the difference. In being willing to add information that would change my viewpoint, I had averted further bad feelings on my part. How much better if I had reserved my opinion until after collecting all the facts in the first place.

Humility helps set aside present feelings, images, and judgments for a while to allow greater objectivity. I do not necessarily negate what I think. I simply shelve it for a while in order to broaden my thinking by listening to others.

When humble, I recognize that my way is not the only way to view situations. Some call such an attitude "having an open mind." It is also humility.

Chapter 9

Learning From Any Experience

"Let the wise listen and add to their learning."—Proverbs 1:5

A S Lynn left church, she was not expecting to have the opportunity of repairing a relationship through a humble, teachable spirit. She walked down the stairs, looking for a few friends to talk with before going home to dinner. Suddenly Floyd blocked her path. The elderly man's words caught her by surprise.

"You just let her drop," he said, his scarlet face screwed into a scowl.

Lynn stared at him, stunned. She felt her face growing redder by the second as she tried to figure out who and what he was talking about. With his short, gray hair he looked the part of an ex-marine drill sergeant. She felt like a new recruit.

"You took her away from me and then just let her drop."

Then she remembered. A few months before, she had wanted to get more involved in some people-oriented activity. Her solitary job left her thirsting to relate to others. The pastors and other church leaders frequently made speeches about the joys of church visitation and the importance of member involvement. She had volunteered to do some visiting, spending some time in Bible study with each person visited.

Barb had been one of those people. A former classmate of Lynn's, she was now married and had several children. After several weeks of studying together with Lynn, Barb wished aloud that her husband would join her in these times of Bible study. "He doesn't even want me to spend time with you studying the Bible," she confided. They had prayed about that together, asking God to give her husband an interest in spiritual things.

The next week Barb wasn't at home at the appointed time. Nor was she there the next week. Lynn didn't believe in pushing things, especially since she knew there was a problem about Barb's husband.

Now as she faced Floyd, she had to admit to herself that maybe she had given up on Lynn a little too quickly. Maybe she should have at least found out why Barb hadn't been home.

"I'm sorry," she said, and walked away as tears filled her eyes. Instead of letting them spill out, she spun out of the parking lot, taking the shortest way home.

Floyd's words rang in her ears, angry and accusing. She wondered if she was really responsible for the loss of a soul, as he had seemed to imply.

Dinner didn't taste very good. The dinner rolls stuck in Lynn's throat. She chewed his words, albeit mentally, more than she chewed the food in front of her.

Why did he have to say that? It's not true. How was I supposed to know I was taking work away from him? He was always talking about involvement. I thought he had more work than he could handle. If the church is full of people like that, who needs it?

"Why, God? Why?" she asked. "I tried to do something useful. He had no right to talk to me like that. What do I do now?"

She tried to read her Bible, searching for an answer. The pain stayed. Slowly, though, over a period of days, another thought grew in intensity above the emotional hurt.

Since he had pointed out her mistake, perhaps Floyd had something to teach her. She would have to ask him to give her some pointers. Though she still felt like giving up on the church, she called Floyd.

He agreed to take her along on one of his visits. The ride seemed a bit strained. She sat quietly in the back seat while he and his wife talked in the front, now and then pausing to ask her a question.

At last, seated in the living room of a family in the downtown area, Floyd pulled out his materials. Lynn had to admit that she had been impressed with his store of knowledge. He had collected magazine articles and newspaper clippings from periodicals published before she was born. He used these to illustrate Bible verses. He presented his material articulately.

On the way home, Lynn expressed her admiration for his collection of information. Even so, she still hesitated to push studying the Bible with Barb if Barb did not want to do it. *God Himself allows people to choose Him*, she thought. They had different styles, Floyd and she.

Floyd's anger, though, seemed to be defused. And her hard feelings of bitterness had been replaced by acceptance and understanding.

A teachable spirit placed Lynn in a nonthreatening position. When Floyd did not feel threatened, he related in a more open and nonthreatening way himself. He no longer had to defend or argue, rant or rave, because Lynn wanted to learn from him.

Even though Lynn did not agree with Floyd, she learned something about the way he thought. Broadening her understanding did not hurt, since she still controlled the choices she made after learning new methods.

What happened to Barb? A few years later she came back to church on her own.

Jesus told His disciples that "the greatest in the Kingdom of heaven is the one who humbles himself and becomes like this child" (Matthew 18:4, TEV). Listen to any preschooler ask a series of "why" questions. Children are eager to learn, to find out about new things.

Adults also find excitement in learning new skills or information. Humiliating experiences, though, carry overtones of devaluation, shattered self-worth, or loss of control. However, viewing these experiences as opportunities for learning can change their impact. The negatives slip away with learning and growth.

As desperate struggling and defensive thinking stop, humility becomes a friend, opening minds, attitudes, and lives to new experiences and viewpoints.

Chapter 10

Looking for Needs

"Each of you should look not only to your own interests, but also to the interests of others."—Philippians 2:4

THE woman staggered through the emergency room door, clutching her chest. "I'm having an asthma attack," she said between gasps.

"Start an IV," the doctor ordered. "Give her aminophylline and morphine." He spelled out the dosages of each.

Frightened by his gruffness—and my first attempt to administer an IV on someone other than people who had let me practice on them—I called for another nurse to be on hand to back me up. I hung the IV supply bottle on its hook, then I looked for the port, a place along the main tubing where I could connect a second tube for the aminophylline. Ten minutes passed.

"Why isn't that IV done yet?" the doctor barked.

My face reddened. Why didn't this tubing have a port? "How fast do you want me to give the morphine?" I asked, intending to give it through the same port, once I found it.

"You mean it's not in the bottle?" His cheeks puffed out slightly as his jaw clamped tighter.

He looked at the patient, who was now breathing normally. "Take out the IV and send her home." He glared at me. I had done everything wrong, or at least too slow. Up until now the patient had received only normal saline, a fluid very similar to the body's own fluid. Yet the patient was better. The doctor said nothing, but I expected even the air to explode any minute. I felt my cheeks burning as I discharged the patient and cleaned up the table and IV equipment. How had he wanted me to do it? I still didn't know. But I knew I had better find out fast.

There are at least two questions to ask when facing a humiliating experience. 1. Does this experience point out an area in which I need to grow? 2. Is God using this experience to show me another person's need?

If the answer is "Yes, I need to grow," as I could answer in my experience with the asthma patient, humility has opened a door to more knowledge, proficient skills, or increased wisdom. In fact, I cannot grow unless I first recognize my need. Humility paves the way to learning.

If I answer yes to the second question, then I create an opportunity to share with God in the experience of loving and giving to another the way He does—based on needs, not necessarily on what anyone deserves.

Jesus illustrated this concept in the story of the vineyard owner who paid his hired men exactly the same wage despite the varying number of hours they had worked. The vineyard owner saw men who needed a full day's wage even though they had not been put to work until late in the day.

Following Jesus' example means looking for others' needs. Those needs may not always be glaring or obvious. Put-downs, domineering or manipulative behavior, all express needs. Dishonesty, stealing, cheating, and many other negative behaviors also point out needs.

The needs could be for acceptance, a good self-concept, love, forgiveness, to trust someone, or any number of deeply rooted needs. People often need just the opposite of what they really deserve.

If I am too busy thinking about how my rights have been trampled, I may miss others' needs. This doesn't mean I will bury hurts deep inside pretending they don't exist. Nor does humility mean that I will let people run over me with unreasonable demands.

If I did that, I would not be filling others' needs; I would be only perpetuating the problem. Humility, though, helps me see beyond my hurts, actively giving to help meet the deeper need.

Zowie had been admitted to our floor as a psychiatric patient. She started the day by demanding her tranquilizer. Now! Two hours before scheduled.

Of course, I could only give it as the doctor had scheduled, but I could talk. She told me of her latest episode. She had smashed all the windows in her boyfriend's car because he decided to move out. During the fight they had destroyed many of the things in her house and smashed the door, leaving the house open to burglars.

After hearing those details, I was surprised to see Zowie's boyfriend visiting her that evening. Sitting on a sofa at the end of the hallway, they talked for hours.

Visiting hours had been over for some time when I finally told them that he would have to leave. Zowie begged for just five more minutes to say goodbye. I agreed.

Ten minutes later I reluctantly went to tell them the time was up. I had hoped Zowie's boyfriend would leave within the time limit on his own. He responded politely and rose to leave.

"Kiss me goodbye," Zowie begged.

"I'm sorry, I have to go," he said.

I agreed.

"Please, just give me a few minutes to say goodbye," Zowie said, turning to me.

"I'm sorry, you've had 10 minutes already, more than I agreed to give you."

Her boyfriend started through the door and down the stairs. She started to follow him.

"Zowie, come back," I said. Psychiatric patients were not allowed off the floor.

"Goodbye, Zowie." Her boyfriend walked down the stairs.

"Now look what you did," she screamed at me. "He left without kissing me. Now we'll never get back together." Hurling profanities in my direction, she stormed through the door and down the stairs.

I followed her, urging her to come back.

"Get out of here," she said. "I never want to see you again."

Following procedure, I called her doctor, who stated that he would not treat her if she left the hospital. I walked down to the parking lot to tell her the doctor's message. Zowie responded with curses. "Get out of here," she said.

Obviously, I was getting nowhere. A male orderly volunteered to stay with her. I watched from the second-story window as they talked in the parking lot. About an hour later Zowie came back to her room and demanded her pain injection. She refused, however, to let me give it.

"That's OK," I said. "I'll ask the other nurse to give it to you." The nurse agreed but told Zowie she would have to wait until she had finished with her regular patients.

The wait must have been too much, because soon Zowie came to me, much quieter, and said, "I guess you can give me my shot."

Calmly I gave the injection.

Her next words caught me by surprise. "How come you're being so nice to me after the way I've talked to you?"

I thought a minute. "I guess, Zowie, I've done things that later I wished I hadn't. Sometimes, in spite of that, people have given me what I needed most—care and concern. I'd just like to pass that on."

Tears filled her eyes. For the rest of the evening she cooperated pleasantly.

People often express their deep needs through negative behavior. As I pray for God to fill those needs, I find my own attitudes changing.

No wonder Jesus said, "Love your enemies, . . . pray for them which despitefully use you" (Matthew 5:44, KJV). I used to read over this verse lightly. I didn't have any enemies. After all, this is an enlightened age of tolerance and peace.

Then I read the verse again. The "despitefully use" part leaped out at me. Maybe that included negative behavior, even though not at the "enemy" level.

Though it might seem strange, I could even take negative behavior as an honor. A person who reacts negatively is, after all, giving out glimpses into his inner self, trusting me with unspoken needs. And with that insight, I can pray, allowing God to work through me to help meet some of those needs.

In helping me see my own needs, humility helps develop greater skills and knowledge. In helping me to see others' needs, humility becomes a tool to develop ways to give love.

Chapter 11

Building Others Up

"Therefore encourage one another and build each other up."
—1 Thessalonians 5:11

HE was an authority in his field of missions. For two hours he presented three components of a theological model that explained how and why cultures relate to religion differently. The audience listened with rapt attention. One could almost hear silent "aha's" and "that explains why I didn't get through."

During the question-and-answer period that followed, one woman stood up and remarked, "I've appreciated what you've said. As I have been thinking, it seems to me that all three of these models are interrelated." She elaborated, and ended by saying, "And the third, to be effective, must come full circle back to the first."

Many speakers would have shifted uncomfortably and said, "That's an interesting point. Ah, yes . . . question over there, please."

But this man had listened intently. When she finished he said, "I wish I had said that. You are right. And in fact, I never saw it until just now."

In responding the way he did, he painted a picture of humility. He had not put himself down. Nor had he tried to maintain his position by ignoring the woman's comment. Instead, he had accepted her at an equal level. Interestingly, his image as a speaker rose. Because he considered learning and understanding more important than his image, we all gained additional insight.

In my mind I contrasted this incident with another. I was backstage, waiting to sing before a religious meeting. The main speaker strutted over to the two other men who would be on stage. "All right, men," he said. "Let's go give these laypeople something to chew on."

They laughed, had prayer, and piously walked onto the platform. The speaker's remark may have arisen from nervous tension. However, someone sitting in the audience might have felt like a puppy being tossed juicy morsels from a superior position.

I could not quite reconcile the "juicy morsels" approach with what I knew about God and the way He relates to His church as a body, with members of different functions but equal importance. To me, building others up means recognizing the special and unique place that God has for each individual. In doing this, I would lose none of my own sense of a unique place. However, in the moment of relating to someone else, I would not be thinking of my own place.

Some people of the Bible seemed to know how to do this. Jonathan befriended David even though he knew David would be king instead of him. John the Baptist announced that Christ would increase while he, John, decreased.

Christ protected the life and reputation of an adulterous woman and told her to go and be free from her sin. In speaking to her this way, He encouraged her to rise to His level.

When Jesus ate with publicans and sinners, He was not trying to prove how humble He was. He ate with them to relate to them on their level and to build them up into freer ways of relating to God.

None of these people acted as they did to gain humility. None put themselves down or denied the place God had given. All simply did their work. Humility came as a natural consequence of focusing on others, on building others up.

My self-esteem helps me see others' abilities and gifts the same way I see my own. Knowing the importance of my own gifts, I can seek to give others that same importance and sense of value through recognizing their gifts.

All this sounds good but humanly difficult. The ego, which governs survival instincts, rebels. If I build others up, even being happy if they become better than I am, they might dominate me. I might end up weak—powerless to control my own life.

God has an answer for ego: Himself. Paul states in Galatians 2:20: "I have been crucified with Christ: and I myself no longer live, but Christ lives in me. And the real life I now have within this body is a result of my trusting in the Son of God, who loved me and gave himself for me" (TLB).

In the Greek, the word for "I" is spelled with three Greek letters: epsilon, gamma, omega. Transliterated, this spells ego, from which our English word comes. Making this substitution, we read, "Ego has been crucified with Christ. Ego no longer lives, but Christ lives in place of ego."

Christ can give more than that survival instinct that keeps me fighting for my position in the world. Knowing that God has a special place for me and that He will make me happy and satisfied in that place can take away the pressure.

Recently I watched as a coworker blossomed and grew with new knowledge and greater responsibilities. Though he was younger and less experienced, I tried to feel happy for him. Yet I felt bored and stagnant in comparison. Why did he get the opportunity to grow?

"God," I prayed, "didn't You say somewhere to 'humble yourselves before the Lord, and he will lift you up'? I think I'm ready to be lifted up."

Silence.

"Uh, God . . . um, You know, I'm kind of humble already. I mean, I'm even writing a book on humility . . ."

I could be wrong, but I think I heard God chuckle a little as He sent His thought voice to remind me that humility is more an attitude toward other people than an attitude about myself.

"Apply what you are writing about," He said. "Build that coworker up."

When I did that, I was free from paralyzing emotions such as fear, disappointment, and envy. I was free to go to my boss and say, "Look, I'm stagnating. How can I find a greater challenge in my work?"

"I didn't realize you were interested in doing more," he said honestly. Together we discussed what I wanted to do. Within a week I had new challenges with some added responsibilities.

And I imagined God looking at me with a twinkle flashing across His eyes, full of understanding. He held out His hand as He said, "See, humility really is a gift. One of My gifts to you."

Chapter 12

"Um, Er-r-r, Praise the Lord"

"Each one should test his own actions. Then he can take pride in himself, without comparing himself to somebody else."
—Galatians 6:4

WE took a really good class on marriage," Kathy said. Her fiancé nodded in agreement.

Kathy continued. "Afterward, I went up and told the teacher how much we appreciated the way he brought spiritual concepts into the class."

Kathy paused and took a breath. "He sort of looked away as if embarrassed and said, 'Well, uh . . . praise the Lord.' "

Many Christians have adopted this phrase as a humble response to congratulations. Sometimes a "Praise the Lord" goes over well among Christians. Other times when it falls flat, people wonder what went wrong. After all, they gave the glory to God.

What are the alternatives? What should we do when people tell us we have done well? Avoid praise by avoiding people? Avoid praise by hiding our talents and spiritual gifts? That would be like the servant in Christ's parable who buried his talent rather than using and increasing it (Matthew 25:14-30). Christ certainly did not praise him.

Every talent and gift comes from God, even if indirectly. I appreciate those gifts because I appreciate God. I value myself because God values me. Yet sometimes Christians

get the idea that accepting praise is wrong, that acknowl-
edging praise will take away humility.

The words on a poster did not agree with that concept.
They said, "Praise makes me humble because I know how
undeserving I am. Praise makes me want to strive to live up
to the praise."

I fear that I am not like the author of that bit of prose;
that, rather than bringing humility, praise will bring pride.
It will if I collect compliments like coins, as our language
suggests in the phrase "to pay someone a compliment."

If Bob gives me a compliment and I think only of myself
and how good Bob must think I am to have given me this
compliment, I actually exclude Bob. This kind of self-focus
leads to pride.

Is it possible to accept praise and yet remain humble?
Yes, if I think of praise as relating instead of collecting. A
compliment from Bob is an expression of his feelings just
as much as any other expression of what goes on inside
him. When I view a compliment in terms of the relationship, the compliment makes me more alert to Bob's
feelings and even to his needs.

At least once, Jesus showed us how to relate to praise in
terms of another person's needs. Nicodemus came to Him
and said, "Rabbi, we know you are a teacher who has come
from God. For no one could perform the miraculous signs
you are doing if God were not with him" (John 3:2).

Nicodemus gave Jesus quite a compliment. First of all,
Jesus was a carpenter, not a rabbi. Second, Nicodemus
stated that Jesus had come from God. Third, he admired
Jesus' miracles. Plus Nicodemus ranked high in Jewish
society.

Jesus could have said, "Thank you, Nicodemus. Coming
from such a person as you, I am honored."

Instead, Jesus realized that men do not come in the
middle of the night just to hand out compliments. Nicodemus had stated that Jesus came from God. Jesus, understanding Nicodemus' need, skipped all the small talk and
got to the point of a spiritual rebirth.

Did Jesus have a perception that we do not have? Probably. Did He have a perception that we cannot have? No. He said that we can have what He had as a gift from God the Father. He can give us that kind of perception on the occasions we need it.

We do not necessarily need to turn every compliment into a spiritual conversation. Our goal is to be sensitive to others and their felt needs.

Often a simple "Thank you" will let another know that we appreciate his expression of the feelings he has shared with us. After all, people honor us with a trust when they open themselves up to us. Looking beyond the praise, receiving it as we would any other giving of self, takes the focus off ourselves.

People often praise in others the things they admire in themselves. A compliment could open a conversation about an area of mutual interest.

Once when I was asked to sing and play my guitar, someone came to me afterward and said, "I really like that finger-picking style you have."

Instead of just saying "Thank you," I added, "Do you play?"

"Yes, I do."

"We'll have to get together sometime," I said. A new friendship was born.

We can keep praise in perspective if we compare accomplishments with our own potential, talents, and most of all, God's plan for our lives.

Paul said, "If anyone thinks he is something when he is nothing, he deceives himself. Each one should test his own actions. Then he can take pride in himself, without comparing himself to somebody else" (Galatians 6:3, 4).

If we compare ourselves with others, we feel either superior or inferior. However, if we compare self with potential, we use different standards of judgment. We stop asking, "How good am I?" Instead we ask, "What is my motive?" Or "Am I using my full potential?" Or "How much good am I doing someone else?"

When we compare ourselves with others, we tend to block our own potential. If we find ourselves superior to another, we do not have to try as hard. If we discover we are not as good as someone else, we are cramped by feelings of inferiority.

However, if we compare ourselves to our own potential, we can be pleased when we master a difficult task. Our weak points, rather than giving us an inferiority complex, motivate us to improve.

A person with a true knowledge of himself or herself knows that talents, accomplishments, and good works are never produced in a vacuum. Each person is indebted to environment, genetics, important people in his or her life, and to God.

Praise gives opportunities to acknowledge indebtedness thankfully. At times "Praise the Lord" may be appropriate if the other person understands this religious jargon.

Of course, if I say "Praise the Lord" while dwelling on how great it is that God can work through me, I am not necessarily humble. The focus may still be on self.

Christ saw people clearly, looking through their praise with such perception, seeking for ways to relate to them, that He was "never elated by applause, nor dejected by censure or disappointment." *

Praise does not need to lead to pride. Praise can lead instead to insights, understanding, and new friendships, as humility gives glimpses of another person through the praise he or she gives.

---

* E. G. White, *The Desire of Ages*, p. 330.

HUMILITY AND THE WORLD

▼

Chapter 13

Serving by Choice

"The greatest among you will be your servant."—Matthew 23:11

I'VE been so busy serving others that I haven't taken time for my own growth," Ed said with a sigh.

Greg looked at him questioningly. "I don't agree with that statement," he said. "We compartmentalize everything. This time is for others, and this other time is for me."

"That's interesting," Ed replied. "What do you mean?"

"Many times I've found I grow most when helping someone else to grow," Greg responded.

How true, I thought. I remembered my student missionary days in Japan. Even though I spent an hour or two preparing for a Bible class, I never overcame a quaking fear just before class began. Yet, time after time, when the class had finished I knew the Holy Spirit had been there helping me teach.

I remember one class in particular. Kazuhiko was one of my more serious upper-level English students who had been reading the Bible on his own. One day in Bible class he asked me, "If God knows everything, including what we are going to do, then how can He give us the freedom of choice?"

I breathed a prayer for help. Then I began to answer. I had spoken only a few words when Kazuhiko interrupted me.

"Oh, I think I understand," he said. "God knows all the possibilities. He knows what would happen to us if we chose any one of the possible choices."

"Yes, that's it," I replied, knowing that I had learned something from Kazuhiko, with the Holy Spirit's help.

Some people think of service to others as dropping a few morsels to a needy soul from a lofty position, then running back to the safety of their own securities. Burnout comes from dropping too many morsels, they think. Once they've given, they think they must be empty. They pull back to get.

Christ pulled back from people during many long nights in prayer—His getting time. Then He spent His days healing and preaching—His giving time.

She was a doctor, a member of the Maryknoll Sisters in Guatemala. We visited her facility to learn about the training program she had for village health workers.

She demonstrated her anatomy lesson. With washable magic markers she drew the major organs of the body on the chest and abdomen of an Indian. I could see why her health worker program succeeded. She taught in a way the people with limited reading ability could learn.

The number of infant deaths had decreased markedly since she had been working with the people, teaching them as they requested it.

"In your work," someone asked her, "how do you keep from getting burned out by constant giving?"

"Those who keep going back to their roots, who keep praying, who keep living the life of faith, will not get burned out by constant giving in social action," she replied.

She paused, sweeping her hand through her blonde hair. "There was a time when I got burned out. I had to take a look at what was happening and why."

She paused again, looking around the room. "Now I am strengthened by the people I work with. I enjoy hearing the

Indians read a text and tell what it means to them. They say some very simple yet profound things that they have learned from meditating on the Word."

Christ also totally immersed Himself in the lives of common people. As He did so, God provided His needs. As a person becomes involved with those in need, recognizing their needs because he recognizes his own, then God can give through giving, even through the very people who are receiving.

No longer is service a duty done from a lofty position. Now service grows out of a bedrock love for humanity and the rest of God's creations. That love leaps into action when it sees any of God's creations hurt or marred. The very expressing of that love works powerfully to fill up and lift up.

Restoring, preserving, and helping God re-create His creations is often a messy, dirty sort of work. An emaciated cancer patient lies nearly helpless in bed, needing to have her bowel movement cleaned up and fresh sheets on the bed. Even more than that, she could use a few words of kindness and encouragement.

A family needs food and clothes. They needed them last month and the month before that. Somehow, all the job possibilities just weren't right for them. Nothing's wrong, really. It seems they've always lived this way.

Papers and plastic bread wrappers blow across the park. Pop cans roll up against the curb. Someone should pick all that stuff up. But what's the fun in that? It's all degrading and hard work. Unless . . .

Unless I do it for love. Humility is the muscle that gets the body of love moving. With humility, I can do all this and more and not mind the doing. Humility frees me to do the nitty-gritty duties that spell out love in actions.

Humility such as this comes from a deep trust in God's ability to give everything needed for survival. If my own needs for esteem, love, and value have been met, I am free to give to others. Trusting that God has met those needs for me (even when I don't feel filled), and trusting that He will fill me with value and self-worth in the future, I can confidently set aside striving to satisfy my own needs. Instead, I will be able to direct my efforts toward helping God fill others with value and self-worth.

I looked down at the 16-page letter in my hand. I could tell from the first paragraph that it wouldn't exactly be a joy to read. I would have thought that after writing a whole stack of similar letters, the writer would run out of criticisms and accusations. At first I had apologized. Then I had tried to defend myself and explain my viewpoint. When the accusations jumped into things I had never even dreamed of doing, I stopped trying to patch things up.

I struggled daily with depression. Just as I would rise above the gloom, another letter would arrive. It almost seemed as if the devil himself was using this experience to attack me and keep me down.

One day I told a friend a little of what had been happening. His reply stuck with me.

"Service to others sometimes helps people rise above things like this."

I started working at the Community Services building one day a week. I volunteered to help Asian refugees in our town find jobs, fill out paperwork, and learn about American housekeeping and life in general.

Showing a Laotian woman how to clean an inch of grease off her stove and oven (and doing most of it myself) was not exactly a "noble" work. My income during this time dipped to an all-time low. Yet those few months were some of the happiest in my life.

Service had helped me put the accusing letters in perspective. People had needs, and I could help. My self-concept rose as I gave. I had no time to waste thinking depressing thoughts about myself that were not even true anyway. Even if the accusations had been true, my service to others would have helped me grow beyond my former self. The accusations would not have remained true, because in God's view our past is forgotten, covered by Christ. What counts is the present.

Service had helped lift me up. I had chosen to serve because I cared. And within that very service, God had given me what I needed.

Chapter 14

Choosing to Enter Another's World

"I have become all things to all men so that by all possible means I might save some."—1 Corinthians 9:22

THE screeching of the cockatoos and the flapping of their wings split the night, which was already humming with millions of mosquitoes and gnats. Crackling fires kept the mosquitoes at bay just enough to let the 200 people sleep in this Bora Bora village in the highlands of Irian Jaya.

But no one was sleeping yet. Tonight the moon was full. "Nana," a woman called from outside the Oosterwals' pole-and-bark home.

The Oosterwals had come here as missionaries. Every day Gottfried Oosterwal talked with the people about Christ, the Bible, and a better way of life. When the tribe moved the village, which was about every six months as food supplies became depleted, the Oosterwals moved with them.

Recognizing the word *friend,* Gottfried's wife, Millie, went to see what the woman wanted. Turning to her husband, her voice tight, she said, "There's a woman out there who wants you to come out and play with her in the full moon."

Wearing only shorts to keep cool, he stood up.

"Gottfried," Millie said, her eyes flashing fire, "at least put on some clothes before you go out to play with that woman."

Though the hot, humid air clung to him, he dressed and went out. The rotting smell of disintegrating vegetation permeated the air as he walked with the woman toward the center of the village.

The Bora Bora tribe viewed life mystically. All of life related to everything else, and uppermost, to the gods. The moonlight especially had great powers for growth. The people planted their gardens by moonlight. With the moon full now, people scurried everywhere, hurriedly placing babies and little pigs in the moonlight. Someone drew a line where the moon's shadow fell. The men lined up behind the line, then the women. One by one they jumped from the dark into the light.

Oosterwal lined up with the rest. And like the rest, he smiled a big, silly grin after he had jumped into the light. Then he went to the back of the line and did it again and again for about two hours.

The ceremony over, Oosterwal walked toward his home. Suddenly he felt a hand on his shoulder.

"Nana," a man spoke.

Oosterwal turned. The man's bare skin glistened in the moonlight. His nosepieces, sticking straight up, cast eerie shadows on his face.

"Nana," the man continued, "now we understand about God."

Puzzled, Oosterwal listened as the man continued.

"We have seen in your life what you have been trying to tell us. You are one with us. We want your God to be our God; your Book, our Book; your people, our people."

The next day the village held a council. The whole village decided to join Oosterwal's church. They said, "Some of the doctrines are difficult to understand, but we have seen that what he speaks is truth."

At their baptism in the life-giving river that flowed 500 yards from the village, Oosterwal spoke about the moonlight as he quoted to them 1 Peter 2:9: "But you are a chosen people, a royal priesthood, a holy nation, a people belonging to God, that you may declare the praises of him who called you out of darkness into his wonderful light."

Would the village have accepted Christianity if Oosterwal had not entered into their world and become a part of them? His love for them, his willingness to join their activities, paved the way for God to work in them.

Actions like these take humility. What would have happened if he had said to himself, "No, I can't go out and play in the moonlight. Number one, my wife will never understand if I walk off with another woman. And then, I might be showing these people that I worship the moon like they do. Besides, it's silly"?

What would have happened if Christ had said, "No, I can't go down to earth. To live among sinners would be to suggest that I condone sin"?

Or what would have happened if, once Christ was here, He had said, "No, I can't eat with Pharisees and tax collectors. After all, a man is known by the company he keeps. The Pharisees are hypocrites, and the tax collectors are cheats"?

Could Jesus have shown the Father's love better by totally separating Himself from the world? He would then have had more time for prayer. He might even have had time to write great books that would have been much clearer than the four incomplete Gospels written by His imperfect followers.

Our greatest challenge is the same one that Jesus took on Himself. He lived fully in the world, yet fully within His Father's better way of life. Only with humility to help us can we do this.

Not everyone can have as positive results as did Oosterwal. However, the possible results must not be the criteria we use to decide whether or not to come close to people. Not all the publicans Christ ate with became His followers. We must find ways of meeting the people who surround us right now on their own turf, where they are comfortable.

I was the only Adventist working with a six-person geological crew in Alaska. Since all of us were from the "lower 48," we spent much of our leisure time together as well as our working time. We visited museums, went rafting, hiked, and shared meals.

Coming to the end of the field season, we planned to say goodbye to each other with a restaurant dinner. One of our crew who could not make the dinner suggested that we meet in a hotel bar for an after-dinner drink.

I knew I would not have to drink alcohol. I would order a 7-Up. But would being seen in such a place represent Christ?

Our socializing would be on a Friday evening, very close to sundown. After eight weeks of doing my share of the Saturday work on Sunday, would I be negating the importance I put on the Sabbath? Would that represent Christ?

There would be no other time to say goodbye to this one crew member. Christ cared about people. Would I represent Christ by going to the farewell occasion?

I remembered Gary, an Adventist geologist who had been in a similar situation of having to decide whether or not to attend a Friday night farewell party for a crew member. He decided to put in a showing for a little while, just to let the man know he cared and that he appreciated him.

A short time later someone found that man's jeep stranded in the desert, with blood spattered in it. Several months later, when Gary told me the story, no one had yet found the geologist. Gary said that he was glad he had gone to the farewell. He would not have had another chance.

I decided to go. As I sipped my 7-Up, I wondered if those who would have chosen not to come would understand this action in terms of loving, caring behavior. Maybe they would see only the rules and my infraction of No. 1098, "Thou shalt not go to bars, especially just before sunset on Friday."

The sun glowed orange on the horizon of Cook Inlet as I said goodbye and excused myself. Nothing dramatic happened. No one died. No one changed beliefs. No one confronted me about my actions.

We might find it easier to enter into another's world if we knew the results would be dramatic. But humility allows us to come close to others because that's what Christ would have done, regardless of the results.

Christ knew that daily He would be surrounded by publicans, tax collectors, the sick, and the common people. Instead of surrounding Himself with a multitude of rules to protect Him from evil, Christ surrounded Himself with influence from His Father acquired through hours of daily prayer.

Christ looked for ways to make spiritual truths strike deep by relating to the daily lives of the people. His motive in everything He did was to reveal the character of God—even when He participated in activities that the "spiritual leaders" thought were not spiritual, such as eating instead of fasting, and healing on the Sabbath.

I learned something about looking for ways to relate to people when, 100 miles into our 1,000-mile trip home from college, Jim pulled out a tape of rock music. "I brought this," he said, "because I'd like to discuss it with you. I'd like to find out what these musicians are really saying—I mean, down deep—and what spiritual needs they are expressing."

I had never listened to rock music this way. As we listened to the tape, we stopped it after each song to discuss the symbolism of the song and what needs the composer might be expressing through his music. Then we tried to think of ways we might approach such a person spiritually.

Entering into another's world may at times be a radical change in another country. At times the results may be dramatic, as they were with Dr. Gottfried Oosterwal. Going into another person's world may also be simply offering empathic understanding, or finding common ground with one who has a different lifestyle or different goals.

Whatever the circumstances, humility lets us set aside preconceived ideas of behavior and enter into someone else's world in love, as Christ would have done. As Paul said, "I have become all things to all men so that by all possible means I might save some" (1 Corinthians 9:22).

Chapter 15

Humility and Power

"He, a giant among men, was but a child before God."
—G. Leibholz

THE tall Man in his early 30s strode into the large building. The noisy bellowing of cows and bleating of sheep almost overpowered the raised voices bargaining for the best price. The stench of manure wafted upward as stressed people stepped hurriedly over little piles on the floor.

"Come on, there. Get moving." A heavy leather whip zinged through the air and slapped down on the rump of a helpless cow. Coins jangled as foreigners exchanged their money for the proper currency, paying a stiff interest rate for the privilege.

The Man gazed around, His serenity contrasting sharply with the confusion. He walked over to the booth nearest Him. In a quiet and meek voice He spoke to the owner. "How's business?"

"What a hassle," the other man growled. "I've got to sell all these doves by the end of the day. Which one do you want?"

"None, for the moment. You know, this is a temple meant for worshiping God. I know you have to make a living, and I know the people need animals to sacrifice. But this isn't exactly the place to sell."

"And who do you think you are?" asked the business-man, scowling and turning away.

"Wait. I have a solution," said Jesus. "I've rented the building across the street. It's roomy enough for everyone here, but far enough away that the noise won't disturb worshipers."

Jesus stepped inside the man's booth. "Here. I'll even help you move. If you'll just take the other end of the table there, we'll have this done in no time."

Wouldn't that have been a more humble way for Jesus to cleanse the Temple? Wouldn't it have even been more "Christian" by our standards?

Amid all the biblical advice to be humble and a servant, God must have had a reason for giving a different picture of Jesus. Instead of acting in a way we usually think of as humble, in this instance Jesus walked into the Temple with a few cords He had made into a whip. When He said "Get out," everyone got out, without even waiting to see how that homemade whip would feel on their backs (John 2:12-16).

The word *power* conjures up pictures of the misuses of power—domination, authoritarianism, dictatorship, one person using another for his own ends, without giving anything in return.

However, power misused does not make all power wrong or out of place in the life of a humble Christian. Just as humility can be a positive force in the Christian's life, power also has a place. Humility and power are not opposites. Jesus had both.

When Jesus walked into the Temple, He found sky-high money exchange rates, and exorbitant prices charged for the "perfect" sacrificial animals. The common people, made poor through the exactment of religious duties, were given a picture of a God that is exacting, demanding, and oppressive.

For the people to see God clearly, these Temple mer-chants had to go. Jesus did not have to use violence. The cords He held above His head signaled authority.

With His piercing gaze and with a ring in His voice, He said "Get out." The merchants suddenly remembered the guilt they had buried deep inside. When Jesus showed His power by matching their authority, their guilt made them leave.

Jesus acted to set people free. The common worshipers could now worship God freely. The merchants too were free—free from their thievery, greed, and guilt. They could choose to remain free or to become enslaved again.

The kind of power that is authority in the face of evil fits well in the lives of humble Christians. Dietrich Bonhoeffer demonstrated this mix of power and humility. During the Second World War he was one of the first to see the true nature of Hitler's ideals. He spoke against national socialism as an attempt to live without God.

After escaping to England, he decided he must go back to Germany, reasoning that he would have no right to minister to his people after the war unless he had shared their sufferings during the war. The Germans captured him. Imprisoned, he helped the sick and depressed.

One sentence perhaps sums up the balance of humility and power in Bonhoeffer's life. "He, a giant before men, was but a child before God." [1]

Bonhoeffer's humility, his willingness to submit to truth no matter what the consequences in his own life, gave him power as a leader.

He never saw the greatness in himself, though. While in prison he wrote a poem describing the vast difference between what he felt about himself and what people said about him. In the poem he wondered which person he was.

The way people think about the power they have makes all the difference. When someone has power mixed with humility, that person sees the needs, the work to be done, and does it.

When someone has power mixed with pride, he or she turns accomplishments inward. Instead of thinking most about needs and how to get a job done, the pride/power person thinks mostly about how many people follow, or what good things others are saying.

"The demon in power is pride," says Richard Foster. "True power has as its aim to set people free, whereas pride is determined to dominate."[2]

This pride is not the same as the pride of a good self-concept, which can be set aside to allow others to experience that same good self-concept. This pride does not include value for others because of the value God puts on self. This pride turns inward, trying to gain value for self and crushing others in the attempt.

Jesus warned against even the seeds of this kind of pride. His disciples had just come back from a great missionary endeavor. Dressed in three-piece suits, they swung their Bibles as their arms moved in rhythm to their confident striding.

"Remember that poor man in the last town?"

"Yes, that was quite a sight. He couldn't even get up."

"And then when I talked to him he answered in the most hideous growl I've ever heard."

"It's the worst case of devil possession I've ever seen."

"Yes, but even that devil fled helplessly before us when we spoke the name of Jesus."

"Isn't it wonderful to be associated with Jesus? We have so much power."

When Jesus heard His disciples talking like this, He told them, "Do not rejoice that the spirits submit to you, but rejoice that your names are written in heaven" (Luke 10:20).

Even though God gives power when needed to set people free, Jesus' value system dictated rejoicing in God, in salvation, rather than in the power. It is as if He is saying, "Use the power when necessary, but don't pay much attention to it. The real power, the stronger power, lies in a humble servant approach."

A dominating power can change outward behavior. Some people may submit with fear and trembling to an authoritarian controller. A dominating power, though, can't touch the inward person. In fact, almost always domination produces either inner or outer rebellion.

A humble servant, however, can approach people's inner lives and deal with their real needs. Lasting choices and changes are made freely without coercion. The humble servant can help provide the support and freedom needed for change. The servant enhances personhood, increases the value of another, liberates inner creativity.

No power is as strong as an inner choice, freely made. Only humility can give the kind of power that sets people free—free to choose, free to grow, free to develop all their potential.

---

[1] Dietrich Bonhoeffer, *The Cost of Discipleship* (New York: Macmillan Co., 1963), p. 12.

[2] Richard Foster, *Money, Sex, and Power* (New York: Harper & Row, 1985), p. 13.

Chapter 16

Humility and Oppression

"Is not this the kind of fasting I have chosen: to loose the chains of injustice?"—Isaiah 58:6

JOSE walked toward us, dressed in brown trousers and nondescript olive shirt. Nothing about his appearance set him apart from any other *campesino* in Guatemala. Yet he was our guide today because he had something special to show us.

"*Vamonos*," he said. "Let's go," he added for those of us who were essentially Spanish illiterates.

Our group of 20 or so piled into an old jeep and the back of a truck. Before coming to Guatemala we had read of the poverty and land problems, and their impact on health and development.

Two days earlier we had sat beside a village, where the men could earn $2 a day if they left to go work on a big coffee plantation. Watching as a woman picked coffee beans from a nearby tree, we listened to the facts.

Guatemala has many natural resources. Every person could be rich. Of the land suitable for cultivation, Guatemala uses only 80 percent. Rural peasants, who make up 80 percent of the population, own only 5 percent of the land being used. Rich landowners, numbering 5 percent of the population, own 95 percent of the land currently being cultivated.

With each generation the problem gets worse. Sons inherit land from their fathers. When the father divides the land between three or four sons, the amount of land per family grows smaller. To feed their families, men are forced to leave for the large plantations.

Today Jose would show us one solution. Bumping along the mountain roads, we saw the postage-stamp-sized plots of land on the steep mountain sides. We stopped beside one of these plots.

Panting for breath, we followed Jose up the hillside and across a terrace of thick grass. A farmer looked up and walked toward us.

After introducing us, Jose said, "This farmer will tell you about his field. He knows more about it than anyone."

The farmer explained about soil erosion, terracing, and a maize crop that would likely be double the average size. All this had happened on one-time marginal land bought cheaply from a rich landowner.

At the next stop we saw a family working in a field of beans. Many families can not afford to buy the beans that, when eaten with maize, would give them a complete protein.

Here again, Jose introduced the peasant farmer, stating, "This farmer knows more about his field than anyone. He will tell you about it."

The Indian peasant told how he had been the first in his village willing to risk trying a new variety of seed and new techniques. Now others had seen his success and had followed suit. Nutrition would improve in this village.

Again we drove, stopped and hiked, this time down into a gully. Here we saw various kinds of fruit trees growing. More than just the staples needed for a family, some of this produce could also bring profits.

Again Jose indicated the farmer. "He will tell you about his farm. He knows more about it than any of us."

Finally, deep in the middle of a field of tall corn with two ears of corn per stalk, Jose stopped and began to tell us something about himself.

He had started as a janitor with the voluntary organization that sponsored this project. Little by little he had learned about new agriculture techniques and had become involved in sharing them with interested farmers.

Rather than being taught by an outside extension worker, farmers teamed up with other farmers like themselves, farmers who had tried the new methods. They learned from each other and from experimenting. The peasants helped themselves.

The newfound self-reliance and confidence aroused suspicions in some, though. The rich landowners thought this was communism. The farmers invited the rich to come and see for themselves what they were doing and even to try their methods. But the rich wouldn't come.

"Jose," someone asked, "with opposition from some, this work must be hard at times. What are your motives for doing it?"

"I have two motives," he said. "First, as a Christian I am my brother's keeper. I must do all I can to help him."

He paused to let his statement sink in. "Second, as a son of God I am a steward of the land. I must take care of it."

As we drove back, anticipating a good supper of black beans and corn tortillas, I knew I had seen more than an agriculture project. I had seen pride on those farmers' faces as they talked about their fields. I had seen more confidence and more self-worth than I had seen in the village where the men went off to work the plantation for a pittance. I had seen success.

In a relationship with God, Christians must fight oppression. Isaiah describes it like this: "Is not this the kind of fasting I have chosen:

to loose the chains of injustice
and untie the cords of the yoke,
to set the oppressed free and break every yoke?
Is it not to share your food with the hungry
and to provide the poor wanderer with shelter—
when you see the naked, to clothe him,

and not to turn away from your own flesh and blood?" (Isaiah 58:6, 7).

Does this mean giving away old, almost-worn-out clothes, food for the baskets at Thanksgiving and Christmas, and money to multiple charities in return for the credit or the dwindling tax deduction? Is this all Isaiah described?

This kind of giving helps most of all when someone encounters an emergency—a house fire, a sudden sickness, a natural disaster.

But another kind of giving better helps the chronic poor and the oppressed. This kind of giving includes the credit for any good accomplished as part of the gift. Only humble givers can also give away the credit.

Oppression has many other causes than lack of material goods. Oppressors treat others the way they do because of prejudice or greed or an unwillingness to understand those they are oppressing.

However, the oppressed too often have nonconstructive attitudes of fatalism (i.e., "It's God's will"), lack of knowledge, or little confidence that life can be any better. When life is rough, the oppressed may find it harder to take risks. After all, if someone tries something new and it fails, life could get even worse.

Many people in various parts of the world today focus on the need to change laws and government policies. Many laws do need to be changed. Daily, news commentators tell of countries whose citizens are crying out for human rights.

Yet, like Jose, we must fight oppression with commitment to a cause. Jose fought oppression not by fighting the oppressors but by fighting the problems oppression caused. He worked to improve the land available.

In the Bible, Isaac fought oppression the same way. When the Philistines started filling in the wells his father had dug, he sent his servants to dig them again. When the Philistines promptly claimed the first one, Isaac said, "OK. No problem." His servants simply dug another well. The

Philistines claimed that one, too. Finally, when they dug the third well, the Philistines gave up (Genesis 26:19-22).

Isaac did not allow the Philistines to dominate him or drive him away. Neither did he go to war over the well. He simply addressed the problem—his household and flocks needed water.

Again Isaiah offers some help as we wonder how to do this task.

"I will put my Spirit on him
and he will bring justice to the nations.
He will not shout or cry out,
or raise his voice in the streets.
A bruised reed he will not break,
and a smoldering wick he will not snuff out.
In faithfulness he will bring forth justice;
he will not falter or be discouraged
till he establishes justice on earth" (Isaiah 42:1-4).

Though Isaiah prophesied about Christ, as brothers of Christ we can expect that God will give us the same abilities and attitudes. Those who oppress others may also be "bruised reeds." Greed and prejudice are slaves of the mind just as much as poverty and malnutrition are slaves of the body. With humility, we may do more to break the barriers of greed and prejudice than all the political clout we might wield.

Simply changing laws will not do everything for the oppressed. Those on top must become willing to give more than a handout; they must also give help in developing new skills and attitudes while giving the credit to those they have helped.

Jose had given the credit for improvements to the respective farmer who owned the land. He had taken no credit for himself, even though he had taught these men and worked with them in their experimental planting.

With such an attitude, Jose had not only given help in solving the food problem, he had also allowed self-confidence to grow. The confidence in being able to solve their own problems may have been the most important thing the farmers gained.

Humility helps in living a positive, growing life. But now humility may start to cost something.

Sometimes I equate being appreciated for gifts, leadership, or knowledge with being valuable. Self-esteem rests in the good done. To think I might give, lead, and create positive changes while never being rewarded can leave me feeling hurt, unless I have first found my supreme value and self-worth in Christ.

Christ worked without thinking of reward. In a relationship with Him, I can also work like He did—quietly recognizing the work God does through me. Then I find that the inner reward satisfies more than any outward praise. I find that humility brings an inner peace that allows me to do far more lasting good for others than before possible.

An old Chinese verse says it like this:

Go in search of your people:
Love them;
Learn from them;
Plan with them;
Serve them;
Begin with what they have;
Build on what they know;
But of the best leaders
when their task is accomplished,
their work is done,
The people all remark:
"We have done it ourselves." *

---

* From David Werner and Bill Bower, *Helping Health Workers Learn* (Palo Alto, Calif.: The Hesperian Foundation, 1982), p. 7.

Chapter 17

Where Do I Get Humility?

"For it is God who works in you to will and to act according to his good purpose."—Philippians 2:13

IN Transylvania, a rich fertile section of Romania bordering Hungary, ethnic Hungarian peasants lost their cottages and gardens to government bulldozers. The dictator Ceausescu decided that Transylvania should be developed into a perfect Communist society, with everyone living in identical small apartments.

The government closed schools that taught in Hungarian. The "systemization" forced peasants to adopt a way of life not their own. Some committed suicide. Others fled across the border to Hungary to save their lives and escape humiliation.

Before, they were humble, living in peace, content with their garden plots in the villages. Ceausescu brought humiliation.

In another country, a girl continues to work quietly in a beauty salon, her long auburn hair pulled back so as not to interfere with the deft movement of her hands. Now and then she pauses to push her glasses up on her nose.

Her eyes narrow slightly as she says, "Trials don't make you humble; they make you hard. I know." She says no more as her hands keep on working.

It's the raw truth in many lives—trials harden, not humble. If humility does not develop from being humiliated, then where does it come from?

Humility is not listed in the Bible as one of the spiritual gifts, and no Bible verse says specifically that God will give humility. Instead, the Bible advises many times, "Humble yourselves . . ." According to *Strong's Concordance*, the word *humble* could often be translated "submit."

"Submit? Oh, no," a person responds. "That's a dirty word. There's no way I'm going to go back to being a trampled-on worm."

Yet Jesus states, "I am gentle and humble in heart" (Matthew 11:29). Jesus is God, the essence of God made understandable to humans. If Jesus is humble, that means that even God is humble. God operates within His own principles of love.

Humility, then, is a choice—a choice to submit to the values that define God and love. Just as God operates within these values, to humble self means to accept those principles and act and make decisions in harmony with them.

To choose the humble way means to be open to others, trying to understand their ways and viewpoint, building others up and seeking to give others added self-worth. A humble person will be able to laugh at some embarrassing situations and learn from others.

A humble person will be able to relate to other people better, because a healthy self-esteem lets self become open to others, their needs and their feelings. In view of the needs of others, humility will allow a person to take risks for the good of others, to use power to set others free and attack the problems of oppression. A humble person will be able to give in this way because he or she trusts God for all needs.

Letting these attitudes take possession of self, submitting to God's way of thinking, brings humility. Submitting does not sound as bad, knowing that Jesus also submits to His own principles of loving, helping, and filling needs.

Submission of this kind does not mean becoming a nonthinker or a nondecision maker. For me to submit means to make decisions within the context of the ideals of the person to whom I have submitted. I will take into account that person's needs, goals, and desires.

Humility, though, is not an all-encompassing submission. God does not ask anyone to submit to evil, but to submit to good in the thick of evil. Sometimes the difference is only a subtle one.

A soldier dressed in dusty, green uniform approaches a man walking along the road.

"Hey, you. Yeah, you in the blue shirt," the soldier yells, pointing his gun at the man. "I want you to carry my pack up this hill."

At this point the man has three choices. He can refuse and be shot. He can accept the pack and grudgingly carry it, all the while thinking about how awful it is that he is being treated this way. Or he can choose the humble way.

"Yes, sir," he replies, "I'll be glad to carry it. In fact, I'll carry it up the next three hills" (Matthew 5:41, very liberal paraphrase!).

By responding this way, the man has taken control of the situation. He has chosen to do good rather than think about "poor me" and how oppressed he is. Instead, he has taken the soldier's demand and turned it into an opportunity to show the soldier the love of God. By doing this, he has taken some of the punch out of the way the soldier wanted to show off his oppressive kind of power.

Humble people never submit to evil—only to God and His values, even in the midst of wrong when wrong is thrust on them. Submitting to God's values is not always easy. However, God promises to help us make that choice. Paul writes, "For it is God who works in you to will and to act according to his good purpose" (Philippians 2:13). Wanting to make the choice is as good as making it, for God will give the power to act.

Humility, then, comes by choice, a choice to submit to God's values, a choice backed by God's Spirit working in the life.